BEAR AWARE

The Quick Reference Bear Country Survival Guide

Bill Schneider

FOURTH EDITION

GUILFORD, CONNECTICUT
HELENA, MONTANA

AN IMPRINT OF GLOBE PEQUOT PRESS

Copyright © 2001, 2004, 2012 by Morris Book Publishing, LLC

A previous edition was published in 1996 by Falcon Publishing, Inc.

FalconGuides is an imprint of Globe Pequot Press.
Falcon, FalconGuides, and Outfit Your Mind are registered
trademarks of Morris Book Publishing, LLC.

Illustrations by Robert Prince based on originals by Kirk Botero.

Text design: Sheryl Kober
Layout: Justin Marciano
Project editor: Ellen Urban

Library of Congress Cataloging-in-Publication Data is available
on file.

ISBN 978-0-7627-7963-5

Printed in the United States of America

10 9 8 7 6 5 4 3 2 1

Contents

Preface
Two Sides to Every Story

"We are apprehensive that as more people make use of the bears' shrinking domain, an increase in bear attacks or maulings might precipitate a reaction that could result in wholesale destruction of the animals."
—Frank C. Craighead Jr.,
famed National Geographic bear scientist

Statistically, you're very safe from bears—but are you safe from statistics?

The answer: Don't rely on statistics, because these numbers can give you false confidence that might prompt you to skip some of the precautions recommended in this book.

Following the advice in these pages will make you safer. Bears definitely add an additional risk to your outdoor adventure, but you take a much greater risk driving to the trailhead. You're much more likely to drown, fall off a cliff, suffer a heart attack or other sudden illness, or succumb to hypothermia on your hike.

Every year, for example, drivers in the United States alone have at least six million auto accidents, some very grisly. These vehicle mishaps claim about 40,000 lives, but the news stories about them hardly make the local front page. On the other hand, any bear mauling, even one resulting in minor injuries, commands banner headlines, which send us a subliminal message that bears are more dangerous than they actually are. This phenomenon won't change, so the bottom line is to keep the danger posed by bears in perspective regardless of how the media covers bear stories.

North America has about a half-million bears, mostly black bears. Yet in our recorded history, bears have killed fewer than 50 people, an average of less than one person per year. For each recorded fatality caused by bears (all species), we have approximately 8 caused by spiders, 13 by snakes, 34 by domestic dogs, 90 by bees and wasps, and 190 by lightning. In the United States alone, domestic dogs bite about 2 percent of the population every year, about five million people, and kill around 25 people per year. Even Western national parks with large grizzly bear populations average fewer than one bear-caused fatality per year, despite the fact that millions of tourists travel through the entrance stations annually.

So, statistically speaking, walking the streets of a big city is more hazardous than walking the trails of bear country. Nonetheless, bears are dangerous. Hopefully, however, with the distribution of more information on how to safely hike and camp in bear country, fewer and fewer bears will make the front page and more and more people will be able to enjoy bear country.

That's our side of the story. There's also the bears' side.

Carelessness can kill not only you or the next person coming down the trail, but also a bear. Most bear attacks, including nonfatal encounters, result in dead bears. Worse, many surprise encounters involve mother bears with cubs, and in far too many cases, both the mother bear and cubs are "removed from the population," which means euthanized or, arguably worse, imprisoned for life without parole in a zoo, research lab, or drive-through wildlife park.

When bears lose their fear of humankind, wildlife managers have little choice but to remove them. In certain circumstances, usually our fault, a bear can gradually become more conditioned to human food or garbage. Once a bear picks up this nasty habit, it's the start of a slow, but virtually guaranteed, death march. Hence the saying, "A fed bear is a dead bear." The bear might avoid its fate for years, but sooner or later it crosses the line and authorities take it out.

Here's the bottom line: Bear encounters obviously pose a threat to human safety, but they also pose a threat to bear safety—and not just the safety of individual bears, but of the entire population. This side of the story doesn't make many headlines, but it's another reason we should take every precaution to avoid an encounter. Too many bloody bear encounters could even lead to a movement to rid the forests of bears.

Therefore, this book has two goals—to save you and a bear.

Dear Bill,

You'd be proud of me. I did it. I just finished a five-day backpacking trip in Yellowstone. And I didn't see a single grizzly, but at night in my tent I heard hundreds of them.

Your friend, Pat

Bear Sense

"*Your best weapon to minimize the risk of a bear attack is your brain. Use it as soon as you contemplate a trip to bear country, and continue to use it throughout your stay.*"

—Stephen Herrero, author of
Bear Attacks: Their Causes and Avoidance

It's difficult to separate bear fact from fiction because bears have a way of proving the experts wrong. As soon as somebody says, "Bears never do this," a bear comes along and does it. So be wary of absolute statements about bears. A typical bear is as mythical as a typical human being.

Knowledge is the best defense. Outdoors people who know about bears also know what equipment to bring, how to set up camp, when and where to hike and be more careful, and which bear and human behaviors increase the chance of an encounter. There is no way to guarantee total safety while traveling in bear country, but the well informed can more easily deal with any encounter and significantly minimize the risk of being injured. Here are the answers to a few of the most commonly asked questions about bears.

Black and Grizzly: What's the Difference?

Although black bears and grizzly bears have significant differences, they share one very notable characteristic: Both species are dangerous and deserve your respect. A common—and serious—mistake is thinking only grizzly bears are dangerous. In fact black bears cause more injuries than grizzly bears do because we have more black bears in more places and because of our nonchalant attitudes toward black bears.

Never view a black bear as "Yogi" or "Smokey." Instead, view black bears as dangerous wild animals. North America has about fifty black bears for every grizzly, but each species is responsible for approximately one-half of the total fatalities traced to bears.

One could interpret this disproportion by saying grizzly bears are more dangerous than black bears, but obviously, both species are dangerous. Alaskan bear authorities, in fact, believe most black bear attacks are "predatory."

Black bears and grizzlies commonly share the same habitat, and sometimes identification can be difficult—another reason to view all bears as dangerous.

Do Bears Stay in the Same Place or Move Around?

Both. Some bears stay close to a specific habitat while others range widely, as much as 50 miles a day. Habitat, reproductive status, and food supply dictate bear movement. Bears usually stay close to a good food source, but never assume "there aren't any bears around here." You can find bears anywhere in their range.

What Do Bears Eat?

Bears are technically called carnivores, but they're primarily vegetarians and probably should be called omnivores—or perhaps, "opportunists"—since they almost always go for the easiest available meal, meat or vegetable. Some studies have found that the majority of a bear's diet is vegetative matter. So you're much more likely to see a bear grazing like an elk than chasing an elk down for dinner.

Along the streams of Alaska and Canada, bears commonly feast on spawning salmon. But in most inland areas, bears feed primarily on foliage, roots, insects, nuts, and berries. Bears hunt and kill large animals, but not as much as you might think, and they also commonly take any opportunity to feed on carrion.

How Do Bears Know Where We Are?

Bears primarily use their sense of smell to detect danger or food, but they also have excellent hearing. Bears have better vision than commonly believed, but they don't use their eyes nearly as much as their nose or ears. Hikers should never assume, however, that bears can smell, hear, or see them. Many environmental situations make it difficult for a bear to detect your presence.

> A leaf fell in the woods.
> The eagle saw it.
> The deer heard it.
> And the bear smelled it.

Why Don't Bears Just Stay Away from People?

They try but they can't, because people are everywhere, even in very remote areas. There are virtually no places left just for bears.

How Do You Know If Bears Are Nearby?

Usually you can't. But bears leave signs such as scat, tracks, diggings, and bark ripped off trees. Familiarize yourself with these signs before going into bear country, but even if you haven't seen any bear sign, don't assume there aren't any nearby. Bears are secretive and wide-ranging and can live near people for long periods without being detected.

GRIZZLY BEAR *(Ursus arctos)*

Color: Black to blond, frequently silver-tipped, giving a grizzled appearance.

Size: About 3 to 4 feet tall at shoulder, often over 6 to 8 feet tall when standing; 200 to 700 pounds in interior areas, and up to 1,200 pounds in coastal areas.

Distinguishing features: Prominent hump over shoulders, sloping back line; dished or concave face, large head; long, curved claws that are usually light-colored and rarely less than 1.75 inches long.

Grizzly Bear Range

Grizzly Bear

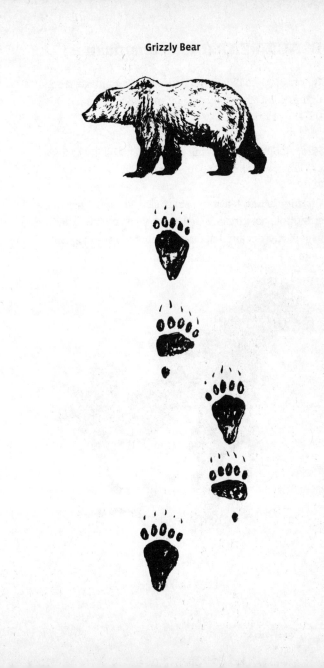

BLACK BEAR *(Ursus americanus)*

Color: Black to blond, but usually with a muzzle that's a lighter color than the body, often with a white patch on the throat or chest.

Size: About 2 to 4 feet tall at shoulder, about 4 to 5 feet tall when standing; 150 to 500 pounds.

Distinguishing features: Small size, straight back line; straight facial profile, small head; shorter claws that are usually dark-colored and rarely more than 1.5 inches long.

Black Bear Range

Black Bear

Bear Mythology: Have You Heard This One?

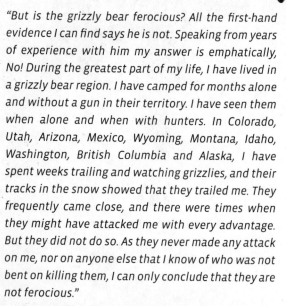

2

"But is the grizzly bear ferocious? All the first-hand evidence I can find says he is not. Speaking from years of experience with him my answer is emphatically, No! During the greatest part of my life, I have lived in a grizzly bear region. I have camped for months alone and without a gun in their territory. I have seen them when alone and when with hunters. In Colorado, Utah, Arizona, Mexico, Wyoming, Montana, Idaho, Washington, British Columbia and Alaska, I have spent weeks trailing and watching grizzlies, and their tracks in the snow showed that they trailed me. They frequently came close, and there were times when they might have attacked me with every advantage. But they did not do so. As they never made any attack on me, nor on anyone else that I know of who was not bent on killing them, I can only conclude that they are not ferocious."

—Enos A. Mills, author of the classic 1919 book The Grizzly: Our Greatest Wild Animal and often considered the father of Rocky Mountain National Park

People die. Bears die. But some of the old myths about bears never seem to die. Some myths have persisted so long that they seem like fact when, in reality, they're either pure fiction or a severe stretching of the facts. Here are a few examples:

Myth: Bears are slow.

Reality Check: Bears sometimes look slow, but that's as far from the truth as you can get. Bears can sprint 35 miles per hour for a short distance, faster than a racehorse and fast enough to run down an elk or deer—and about twice as fast as the fastest human sprinter.

Myth: Bears can't run downhill.
Reality Check: Bears can run extremely fast uphill and downhill. Just because bears have shorter front legs certainly doesn't mean they have trouble running in any terrain.

Myth: Bears can't climb trees.
Reality Check: Actually, mature grizzly bears can climb almost any tree (even trees with branch-free trunks), but they rarely do so, probably because it's difficult. If you can easily climb the tree, a grizzly bear probably can, too. Mature grizzlies can also reach 15 feet up a tree, young grizzlies with sharper claws can easily climb trees, and all black bears can proficiently climb trees—and frequently do.

Myth: Bears can't see.
Reality Check: As far as scientists can determine, bears can see about as well as humans can. One theory suggests that bears commonly see better when young and suffer from failing vision in old age. Sound familiar?

Myth: Bears are afraid of dogs.
Reality Check: Some dogs chase bears, but most dogs lying around the house most of the year waiting for those one or two weeks when they can come along to "protect" you on your outdoor vacation are not "man's best friend" in bear country. Bears commonly chase or kill dogs, an excellent reason not to take Fido on your wilderness trek.

Your dog might run across a bear, the bear could chase your faithful pet back to its master, and then, of course, you have a big problem. Any dog in bear country must be carefully controlled and not allowed to run free.

Most national parks, incidentally, prohibit dogs in the backcountry.

Myth: Black bears aren't dangerous.
Reality Check: All bears are dangerous, but statistically, black bears may be more dangerous than grizzly bears. Black bears have injured and killed at least as many people as grizzlies have, and they've been responsible for some of the most predatory attacks and gruesome fatalities. Black bears also inhabit more areas than grizzlies do, increasing your chances of encountering a bear.

Myth: Bears aren't found around developed areas.
Reality Check: You might find more bears around developed areas than you would in the remote backcountry. Bears can be very secretive, so just because you haven't seen bears around a developed area, doesn't mean they aren't there. Keep in mind that humans gravitate to the same high-quality habitat that bears do. We put our settlements along streams, in low country with rich soils and diverse vegetation, so bears and humans like the same places.

In addition, some local residents and commercial establishments might still be careless with garbage, allowing bears to feed on it. In some tourism developments, proprietors of hotels and restaurants actually feed bears on purpose to attract bear-watching tourists. These circumstances could make developed areas more dangerous than the deepest wilderness.

Myth: Bears don't use trails.
Reality Check: Bears frequently use trails because they offer the path of least resistance. You wouldn't fight through thick underbrush when you could use a well-maintained trail, so why would a bear?

Myth: Bears only come out at night.
Reality Check: Bears are usually more active around dusk and dawn, but they can be active anytime during the day or night, especially on cool, wet days or during the early spring or late fall.

Myth: Bears can't swim.
Reality Check: Bears love water and are excellent swimmers.

Myth: Horses attract bears.
Reality Check: Nobody knows if horses attract or deter bears (or neither), but horses normally make more noise and put out more smell on the trail than hikers do. Horses also sense bears before we do, so it's more likely that horses are a deterrent.

There isn't a single recorded incident of a backcountry traveler being mauled by a bear while riding a horse. However, a few people have been hurt after being thrown from a horse spooked by a bear. Horse food or pellets can definitely attract bears.

Myth: Smoke from campfires attracts bears.
Reality Check: There is no scientific evidence to support this theory, nor have there been any encounters linked to campfire smoke. It's just as likely that campfire smoke serves as a deterrent by alerting bears for miles around of your presence. However, cooking over a campfire (as

opposed to a backpacking stove) could disperse food odors more widely and, perhaps, attract bears. Also, partially burned food in fire pits attracts bears. Never burn leftovers unless you're positive the campfire will stay hot enough long enough to completely burn all food and destroy odors.

Myth: Bears are always afraid of people.
Reality Check: Most bears are indeed afraid of people—or at least try hard to avoid us—but there are exceptions. Bear populations in some national parks may be gradually losing, generation by generation, their fear of humans. Each year, a few bears display behavior that clearly shows they have lost their fear, which makes them more dangerous.

Hiking in Bear Country

3

"Are grizzly bears killers? I would have to say no. If the grizzly bear were half as bad as commonly portrayed, early explorers and frontiersmen would not have gotten far across the prairies, and the opening of the West would likely have been delayed until the advent of the repeating rifle."

—Andy Russell, famous Canadian conservationist and author of Grizzly Country and many other books

The first step of any hike in bear country is an attitude adjustment. Nothing guarantees total safety. Hiking in bear country adds a small additional risk to your trip. However, minimize that risk by adhering to this age-old piece of advice: Be prepared. And being prepared doesn't only mean having the right equipment. It also means having the right knowledge, which, again, is your best defense.

Letting Fear Ruin Your Trip

Don't be the hiker who describes his or her recent backpacking vacation like this: "I didn't see a single bear, but I heard hundreds of them at night while lying sleepless in my tent."

You can—and should—thoroughly enjoy your trip to bear country. Don't let the fear of bears ruin your vacation.

This fear can accompany you every step of the way. It can constantly lurk in the back of your mind, preventing you from enjoying the wildest and most beautiful places left on Earth. And even worse, some bear experts think bears might actually be able to sense your fear.

Being prepared and knowledgeable gives you confidence. It allows you to fight back the fear that can haunt you throughout your stay in bear country. You won't—nor should you—forget about bears and the basic rules of safety, but proper preparation allows you to keep the fear of bears at bay and let enjoyment rule the day.

Being Totally Safe?

If we really wanted to be totally safe, we probably would never go hiking—bears or no bears. We certainly wouldn't—at much greater risk—drive hundreds of miles to get to the trailhead. Perhaps a tinge of danger adds a desired element to our wilderness trip.

The Basic Rules of Safely Hiking Bear Country

Nobody likes surprises, and bears dislike them, too. The majority of bear maulings occur when a hiker surprises a bear. Therefore, it's vital to do everything possible to avoid these surprise meetings, starting with "The Basic Five":

1. Be alert.
2. Hike in a group and stay together.
3. Stay on the trail.
4. Hike in the middle of the day.
5. Make noise.

If you follow these five rules, your chance of encountering a bear on the trail narrows to the slimmest possible margin.

No Substitute for Alertness

As you hike, watch ahead and to the sides. Don't fall into the all-too-common and particularly nasty habit of fixating on the trail a few feet ahead. It's especially easy to do this when dragging a heavy pack up a long hill or when carefully watching your step on a rocky or eroded trail.

Using your knowledge of bear habitat and habits, be especially alert in areas most likely to be frequented by bears, such as avalanche chutes, berry patches, along streams, through stands of whitebark pine, and in salmon-spawning areas.

Watch carefully for bear signs and be especially watchful (and noisy) if you see any. If you notice a track or scat but it doesn't look fresh, pretend it's fresh. The area is obviously frequented by bears.

The Wind

The wind can be friend or foe. The direction and strength of the wind can make a significant difference in your chances of encountering a bear. When the wind blows on your back, you're much safer, since your smell travels ahead of you, alerting any bear on or near the trail ahead. Conversely, when the wind blows in your face, your chances of a surprise meeting with a bear increase, because a bear can't smell you coming, so make more noise and be more alert.

A strong wind can also be noisy and limit a bear's ability to hear you coming. If a bear can't smell or hear you coming, the chances of an encounter significantly increase, so watch the wind.

Safety in Numbers

There have been very few instances in which a large group has had a serious encounter with a bear. Instead, most hikers mauled by bears were hiking alone or with one other person.

Large groups naturally make more noise and put out more smell and probably appear more threatening to bears. In addition, if you're hiking alone and get injured, there's nobody to go for help. For these reasons, some national parks recommend or require parties of four or more hikers when going into bear country.

If a large party splits up, it becomes two or more small parties or a group of solo hikers, and the advantage is lost. So stay together.

If you're on a family hike, keep the kids from running ahead or trailing behind. If you're in a large group, keep the stronger members from going ahead or weaker members from lagging behind. The best way to prevent this natural separation is to ask one of the slowest members to lead. This keeps everybody together.

People and Trails

Although bears use trails, they don't often use them mid-day when hikers commonly use them. Through generations of associating trails with people, bears probably expect to find hikers on trails, especially during the middle of the day. On infrequently used trails, however, it may be more likely to find a bear using the trail or bedded down near the trail.

On the other hand, bears probably don't expect to find hikers off trails. Bears rarely settle down in a day bed right along a well-used trail. However, if you wander around in thickets off the trail, you might stumble into an occupied day bed or cross paths with a traveling bear.

Sleeping Late

Bears—and most other wildlife—usually aren't active during the middle of the day, especially on hot summer days. Many wild animals, including bears, are most active around dawn and dusk. Therefore, hiking early or late increases your chances of seeing wildlife, including bears. Likewise, hiking in the middle of a hot day reduces the chance of an encounter.

Being Loud and Obnoxious

Perhaps the best way to avoid an encounter is to make sure the bear knows you're there, so make lots of noise. However, the best type of noise is a source of debate.

One theory supports metallic noise—such as bear bells chiming, an aluminum fly rod case or metal-tipped walking stick clanging on trailside rocks, or pebbles rattling in a can—as the best. Metallic noise doesn't occur in nature, so it must come from humans, the theory goes, and is less likely to be muffled by natural conditions than human voices.

Other bear experts, however, think that human voices or loud clapping rather than metallic noise are more likely to alert bears of your presence. One recent research project in Alaska found that bears more or less ignored both metallic noise (bear bells) and human voices unless these sounds were unusually loud, but were alerted immediately by the sound of snapping sticks and bearlike growls. Loud clapping tends to sound like twigs breaking and has been effective in alerting bears.

All bear experts recommend making noise, but you have to make the decision on what type of noise. One way to make the decision easier is to check at the local ranger station, which often gives out specific recommendations.

Not Being Loud and Obnoxious

While planning your noisemaking, be sure to discuss respect for other hikers—or as some experts call it, "appropriate noise." Hikers hike to get away from "noise pollution," so keep in mind that some conditions warrant silence to better enjoy wild nature. For example, if you're closely following another group of hikers up the trail, you can forgo noisemaking. The same goes in places where there's no chance of seeing a bear, such as open stretches of trail through tundra or alpine meadows or trails gouged out of cliff faces where you can see a long distance up the trail.

You can safely remain quiet and enjoy the wilderness in these situations and then revert to noisemaking when you approach a thicket or brushy ravine. Also, please preserve everybody's wilderness experience by not making loud noises in camp.

A Better View
If you see a bear, don't try to get closer for a better look. The bear might interpret this as an act of aggression and charge.

A Long Lens Instead
A high percentage of people mauled by bears are photographers. That's because they're purposely being quiet, hoping to see wildlife. In some cases they try to get closer to a bear for a better photo. Such behavior is counter to all rules for traveling safely in bear country—and threatens the bear, too, which is often killed after being involved in a serious encounter.

Running Up the Risk
Many avid runners like to get off paved roads and running tracks and onto backcountry trails. But running on trails in bear country can be seriously hazardous to your health.

Most runners avoid running during the heat of the day. Instead, they run early or late in the day when bears are most active. Runners rarely make enough noise when running, and they might even sound like a wild animal (i.e., bear food) running on a trail.

Experienced trail runners know that you tend to get closer to wildlife running than you do walking. Some people think that's because you cover distance faster than expected by wildlife. Other people think it's because you tend to be quieter when running.

Whatever the reason, running on trails obviously increases your chance of surprising a bear. The best advice is to avoid running in bear country, but if you're a hopelessly addicted runner and can't resist trying a scenic trail in bear country, at least strap a bell on your fanny pack, take bear pepper spray, and run during the heat of the day.

Hiking after Nightfall

Like running on trails, hiking at night can be very risky. Bears are often more active after dark, and you're less likely to see them until it's too late. If you get caught out at night, be sure to make lots of noise.

Dead Meat

If you see or smell an animal carcass when hiking in bear country, immediately vacate the area. Don't let your curiosity keep you near the carcass a second longer than you need to recognize this as an extremely dangerous situation.

Bears commonly hang around a carcass, guarding it and feeding on it for days until it's consumed. Your presence could easily be interpreted as a threat to the bear's food supply, and a vicious attack could be imminent.

If you see a carcass ahead of you on the trail, don't go any closer. Instead, abandon your hike and return to the trailhead. If the carcass is between you and the trailhead, take a long detour around it, upwind from the carcass, making lots of noise along the way. Be sure to report the carcass to the local ranger or game warden. This tip might prompt a temporary trail closure or special warnings but might also prevent injury to other hikers and the death of a bear. Rangers will, in some cases, go in and drag the carcass away from the trail, but usually they temporarily close the area.

Cute, Cuddly, and Lethal

The same advice for approaching carcasses goes for bear cubs. If you see one, don't go one inch closer. The cub might seem abandoned, but it is not. Mother is nearby, and female bears fiercely defend their young.

Side Trips

Many backpackers like to take a side trip during a long day to see a special place or enjoy a few hours without the heavy pack. If you do this, be sure to hang your pack out of the reach of bears in much the same manner as you would hang your food at night. If you don't take the time to do this, you might end up with, at the least, a destroyed backpack or, at the worst, an encounter with a bear defending the food reward it found in your pack.

You could also be doing a great disservice to future backpackers by conditioning a bear to look for food in backpacks. And once again, the result would be a dead bear.

As a fringe benefit, you won't have holes chewed in your pack by rodents.

THE BEAR ESSENTIALS:
Hiking in Bear Country

Knowledge is the best defense.

There is no substitute for alertness.

Hike with a large group and stay together.

Don't hike alone in bear country.

Stay on the trail.

Hike in the middle of the day.

Make lots of noise.

Never approach a bear.

Cubs are deadly.

Stay away from carcasses.

Know and adhere to regulations.

Over-regulated?

Nobody likes rules and regulations. However, national parks and forests have a few that you must follow. These rules aren't meant to suck the freedom out of your trip. They're meant to help bring you back safely—and to keep bears wild and alive.

When you get a backcountry camping permit in a national park, you get a list of these rules. In some cases, they're printed right on your permit. In national forests you usually don't need a permit, but you can check with the local ranger for any special regulations.

In both national parks and national forests, carefully read the notices on the information boards at trailheads.

No Bears!

Now you know that to reduce your chance of a close encounter with a bear while hiking to the smallest possible margin, you'd have to walk up the trail constantly clapping or clanging two metal pans together. You probably wouldn't see a bear (or any other wild animal, for that matter), and you'd ruin your wilderness experience. You left the city to enjoy nature and escape such noise.

How safe can you be while still enjoying your trip? It's a balancing act. Be knowledgeable and then decide what precautions to take. Everybody has to make his or her own personal choice. If you follow all bear awareness recommendations in this book religiously, you probably won't see any bears. Most people would relish the opportunity to see a bear in a wild setting and at a safe distance. If you want to see wildlife, including bears, make noise only when you're in situations where you're likely to surprise a bear at a dangerously close distance.

Camping in Bear Country

4

"Already our studies were revealing that the grizzly did not fear man but preferred to avoid him when possible and, as other bear–man confrontations showed, to combat him if necessary."

—Frank C. Craighead Jr., famed National Geographic bear scientist

Staying overnight in bear country is not dangerous, but it adds a slight additional risk to your trip. The main differences between day trips into bear country and camping in bear country are more food, cooking, and garbage. Plus, you're in bear country at a time when bears are commonly most active. Once again, however, following a few basic rules greatly minimizes this risk.

Local Knowledge

Most national parks require backpackers to have a backcountry camping permit. One reason for this system is safety. If a bear has been raiding camps in one area in the park, rangers probably won't allow any overnight camping there. Backcountry campsite reservation systems also provide an opportunity to discuss the bear situation with a knowledgeable ranger. After you select a campsite, ask the ranger about bear activity in the area. In most parks, you get a brochure or can watch a short video on camping in bear country.

Land managers for most national forests and other public lands don't require permits or designate campsites, but it's always wise to stop in at the local ranger station and ask about bear activity before heading for the trailhead.

A Bear Unfriendly Campsite

Since bears and people often like the same places, selecting a good campsite is a key decision.

Sometimes, you have little to say about where you camp. If you're backpacking in a national park, regulations probably require that you stay in a precisely located campsite reserved in advance. The National Park Service (NPS) considers the bear situation when designating campsites, and discussing it with the ranger might prompt you to choose one site over another.

In most national forests and some national parks such as Yosemite and Denali, you can camp anywhere. Regulations might require you to camp certain distances from water or trails, but you aren't confined to a specific campsite.

When you find your campsite, immediately think bears. Look around for bear sign. If you see fresh sign or see a bear nearby, don't camp there—even if you're in a national park and you have reserved this campsite. If you have time before nightfall, return to the trailhead and report the incident to a ranger. If it's getting late, you have little choice but to camp at an undesignated site and report it to the ranger after you finish the hike. Safety always prevails over regulations. Don't get yourself in a situation where you have to hike or set up camp in the dark.

Being careful not to camp in a site frequented by bears is perhaps the most important precaution you can take. Unfortunately, people who cause a bear to become conditioned to human food or garbage are rarely the people who suffer the consequences of their misdeeds.

The person who is injured usually comes along later and unknowingly camps in the same site where a bear has become accustomed to getting human food.

Also look for signs of previous campers. If you find food scraps, litter, or other signs that the previous campers didn't use proper bear-country camping techniques, consider choosing a different campsite.

It's very important to plan your hike so you aren't setting up camp a half hour before nightfall, which doesn't leave time to move to another campsite if necessary. If you set up camp in the dark, you have little chance to check around for bear sign or evidence of previous campers.

A Good Campsite

A key feature of any good campsite in bear country is a place to store food. Most designated sites in national parks and in some national forests have a food-storage device such as a "bear pole" or metal bear-resistant food-storage locker. However, in most national forests and other public lands, even in some national parks, you're on your own for storage of food and garbage, so scout the campsite for trees where you can hang your food and garbage. You need a tree at least 100 yards from your tent site with a large branch, or two trees close enough to suspend your food between them on a rope. You can also use a tree that has partially fallen and is still leaning securely on other trees. In any case, however, the trees must be tall enough to get the food at least 10 feet off the ground and 4 feet from the tree trunk.

Choose a campsite away from popular fishing areas such as along salmon-spawning streams or lake inlets. If previous campers fished close to camp, they may have left dead fish or fish entrails around camp, and the smell of fish definitely attracts bears. If you have fish for dinner, clean them at least 200 yards from camp and dispose of the entrails by throwing them into deep water.

Avoid camping along trails, streams, or lakeshores, which often serve as travel corridors for bears. Since bears like to travel and remain concealed in trees, camp on the edge of an open area and, if possible, set your tent near an "escape tree" that you can climb in case a bear comes into camp, and make a mental note of its location so you can find it at night. Pick a tree that's not too easy to climb; you don't want it to be easy for the bear.

Setting Up Camp

Once you've found a good campsite, take the next crucial step of correctly setting up camp, which isn't as simple as it sounds. Some camping traditions can increase the chance of a bear entering your camp.

You probably have seen photos of picturesque camping scenes with a family just outside the tent entrance sitting around the fire cooking dinner. Forget this. The sleeping area and the cooking area must be separated.

Set up the tent at least 100 yards upwind from the cooking area. Also, if possible, pitch the tent uphill from the cooking area. Since night breezes in the mountains usually blow downhill, the wind will carry food smells away from the sleeping area instead of over it.

Spreading out the camp might create some extra walking and inconvenience, but if a bear comes into your camp, it's likely to go straight for the smell of food—where you've been cooking and eating. So, obviously, you don't want to be sleeping near there. Concentrate all food smells in the cooking area and keep them away from your sleeping area.

Get in the habit of separating cooking-area and other fragrant items from sleeping-area items in your backpack, so you can easily divide them once you make camp.

For large parties, set up tents in the most secure areas and space them out linearly. Put the most experienced people at each end of the line of tents. Hikers who plan to stay up most of the night listening for bears get the inside spots.

Free Sleeping

A few national park visitors have been known to have a particularly bad habit called "free sleeping." In an attempt to save money or when all the campgrounds are full, some visitors simply pull off the road in an undesignated camping area and pitch a tent or, even worse, just throw a sleeping bag out on the ground.

Besides violating park regulations, this can be very dangerous. The "free sleeper" might be saving a few dollars, but he or she might also be unknowingly camping in an area heavily used by bears.

Under the Stars

Some people prefer to sleep out under the stars instead of using a tent. This might work in areas not frequented by bears, such as desert environs, but not in bear country. The thin fabric of a tent certainly isn't any real physical protection from a bear, but it does present a psychological barrier.

Storing Food and Garbage

In many designated campsites, rangers have strategically placed a "bear pole" or metal food storage locker near designated cooking areas. If the campsite doesn't have an official food storage device, be sure to find a good tree for hanging food and garbage before it gets dark. Storing food after darkness falls isn't just difficult—it also makes it easier to forget some juicy morsel on the ground.

Even better, use a bear-resistant food storage container (BRFC). Based on a growing emphasis on keeping human food and garbage well away from bears, several manufacturers have, with encouragement from agency wildlife managers, started selling these portable containers. They're light, fit conveniently in backpacks, and most models have been tested with captive bears to make sure even the most aggressive bruin can't get inside. Some national parks require backpackers to use BRFCs, and using them anywhere in bear country is a good idea.

Putting double-bagged food and garbage into a BRFC gives you triple protection. To be even more careful, hang the BRFC or put it in the metal food-storage locker, if your campsite has one. At the very least be sure to leave it near the cooking area at night and nowhere near the tents.

In addition to storing food and garbage properly, try hard to keep food odors off your pack. If you fail, you can put the food bag and garbage inside and hang the pack. Be sure to store scented items such as toothpaste, sunscreen, bug dope, and water bottles (especially if used for juice, lemonade, or fitness drinks) along with food and garbage.

Unforgettable Items

Setting up your campsite for proper storage of food and garbage requires a few essential items. It's a good idea to make a checklist before you leave home, so you don't

A model campsite for camping in bear country.

forget to bring any of them. For starters, pack ziplock bags for storing food and garbage: They keep food smell to a minimum and keep food odors off your pack, clothing, and other gear. You'll also need a special bag (sturdy and waterproof) for hanging and storing food. You can get drybags at most outdoor retailers, but you can get by with a trash compactor bag. Regular garbage bags are too flimsy and can break and leave your food spread on the ground.

Even when using a BRFC, keep food stored in ziplock bags.

If not using a BRFC, you'll also need 100 feet of nylon cord for hanging food and garbage. You don't need a heavy climbing rope; go light instead. Parachute cord will usually suffice unless you plan to hang large quantities of food, garbage, and gear, which could be the case on a long back-packing excursion with a large group.

You can also buy a small pulley system to make hoisting a heavy load easier. Again, you can usually get by without this extra weight in your pack unless you have a massive load to hang.

Getting It Up There

People get hurt hanging food and garbage, so be careful.

The classic method is tying a rock or piece of wood to the end of your rope and tossing it over the branch and then attaching the rope to the bag or backpack and hoisting it up 10 feet or more. If the load gets too heavy, wrap the rope around a small tree or branch for leverage.

To make hanging food easier, take a small ditty bag and permanently attach at least 50 feet of nylon cord to it. Then, when you're at camp, instead of trying to tie a rock on the end of your rope, put rocks or sand in the small bag, close it, and toss it over the branch or bear pole.

Use gloves to avoid rope burn. And, of course, don't let the rock or wood come down on your head—it happens! Also, don't let anybody stand under the bag until you're sure it's securely in place.

Also, be careful not to leave your rope behind the next morning. Once you've untied your food, slowly pull your rope over the branch. Don't jerk it. If the rope gets stuck and you can't climb the tree, you have to leave it behind.

What to Hang

Hang or store everything that has any food smell. This includes cooking gear, eating utensils, water bottles, bags used to keep food in your pack, garbage, and even clothes with food smells on them. If you spilled something on your

Steps for hanging food and garbage between two trees.

Steps for hanging food and garbage over a tree branch.

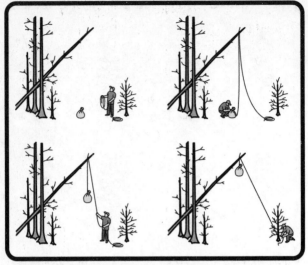

Steps for hanging food and garbage over a leaning tree.

clothes, change into other clothes for sleeping and hang those smelly clothes with the food and garbage. If you take them into the tent, you aren't separating your sleeping area from food smells.

Also, hang or securely store scented nonfood items like toothpaste, bug dope, and sunscreen.

Hanging or storing food at night isn't the only storage issue. Also make sure you place food correctly in your pack. Use airtight packages as much as possible. Store food in the containers it came in or, once opened, in ziplock bags. This keeps food smells out of your pack and off your other camping gear and clothes.

In the Tent
You can't be too careful about keeping food smells out of the tent. If a bear has become accustomed to foraging for

food at that campsite, it's vital for your protection to keep all food smells out of the tent. This often includes your pack, which is hard to keep odor-free, and the clothes you used for cooking and eating.

Usually, only take valuables (such as cameras and binoculars), clothing, and sleeping gear into the tent—and, of course, bear spray. Also, keep a flashlight or headlamp in the tent. If an animal comes into camp, you need light to identify it.

The Campfire

Regulations prohibit campfires in many areas, but if you're in a place where fires are allowed, treat yourself. Besides adding to the nightly entertainment, a campfire can make your camp safer from bears.

The campfire provides the best possible way to get rid of food smells—as long as food scraps and garbage are totally burned away to ashes. Build a small but hot fire and burn everything that smells of food—garbage, leftovers, fish entrails, everything. if you brought food in cans or other incombustible containers, put them in the fire, too. You can even dump extra water from cooking or dishwater on the edge of the fire to erase the smell.

In the crowded wilderness of today, campfires are rarely in line with the principles of zero-impact camping. However, if you decide bear safety outweighs the leave-no-trace ethics, be sure you have the fire hot enough to completely burn everything. If you leave partially burned food scraps in the fire, you're setting up a dangerous situation for the next camper who uses that campsite.

Before leaving camp the next morning, dig out the fire pit and pack out anything that hasn't totally burned, even if you believe it no longer carries food smells. For example, many foods like dried soup or hot chocolate come in foil packages that might seem like they burn, but they really don't. Pack out the scorched foil and cans (now with very minor food smells). Also, pack out foil and cans left behind by other campers.

Burning leftovers in campfires is not allowed in some national forests and national parks, so check local regulations before heading for the trailhead. In most cases, you'll find the best advice listed prominently on the trailhead information board, which is, "Pack it in. Pack it out."

Types of Food

Don't get paranoid about the types of food you bring. All food has some smell, and you can make your trip much less enjoyable by fretting too much over food.

Perhaps the safest option is freeze-dried food. It has very little smell, and it comes in convenient envelopes that allow you to cook it by merely adding boiling water, so you don't have cooking pans to wash or store. However, freeze-dried food is expensive, and many campers don't use it—and still safely enjoy bear country.

Dry, prepackaged meals (often pasta- or rice-based) offer a more affordable alternative to freeze-dried foods. Also, take your favorite high-energy snack and don't worry about it. Avoid fresh fruit and canned meats and fish.

What food you bring is much less critical than how you handle it, cook it, and store it. A packet or can of tuna, for example, might put out a smell, but if you eat all of it in one meal, don't spill it on the ground or your clothes, and burn the can or store it in an airtight bag later, it can be quite safe.

How to Cook

The overriding philosophy of cooking in bear country is to create as little odor as possible. Keep it simple. Use as few pans and dishes as possible.

Except for weather emergencies, never cook in the tent. This creates food odors in the tent (the last thing you want when in bear country) and you could set your tent on fire.

If you can have a campfire and decide to cook fish, try cooking in aluminum foil envelopes instead of frying or roasting the fish over an open flame. Then, after removing the cooked fish, quickly burn the fish scraps off the foil. Using foil also means you don't have to wash a pan.

Also, manage fuel for your backpacking stove carefully. Fuel can be a strong bear attractant. Use a funnel and no-spill container when refilling stoves.

Another Reason to Dislike Leftovers

Try hard not to cook too much food, so you don't have to deal with leftovers. If you end up with extra food, you only have two choices: carry it out or burn it. Definitely do not bury it or throw it in a lake or leave it anywhere in bear country. A bear will find and dig up any food or garbage buried in the backcountry.

Taking Out the Garbage

In bear country you have only two choices for dealing with garbage—burn it or carry it out. Plan ahead and prepare for garbage handling. Bring along ziplock bags to store garbage, and generate as little garbage as possible by discarding excess packaging beforehand at home.

Bears are attracted to garbage no matter where it is, so make sure you pack out everything you pack in—and leave a clean camp.

Washing Dishes

This is a sticky problem with only one easy solution—if you don't dirty dishes, you don't have to wash them. Try to minimize food smell by using as few dishes and pans as possible—or better yet, none at all. If you use the principles of zero-impact camping, you're probably doing as much as you can to reduce food smell from dishes.

If you brought paper towels, use one to carefully remove food scraps from pans and dishes before washing them. Then, when you wash dishes, you'll have much less food smell. Burn dirty towels or store them in ziplock bags with other garbage. Put pans and dishes in ziplock bags before putting them back in your pack.

If you end up with food scraps in the dishwater, drain out the scraps and store them in ziplock bags with other garbage, or burn them. You can bring a lightweight screen to filter out food scraps from dishwater, but be sure to store the screen with the food and garbage. If you don't have a screen, use your bandana. If you have a campfire, pour the dishwater around the edge of the fire. If you don't have a fire, take the dishwater at least 100 yards downwind and downhill from camp and pour it on the ground. Don't put dishwater or food scraps in a lake or stream.

Also, don't put it off. Do dishes immediately after eating to minimize food smells.

Finally, although this possibly runs counter to accepted rules of cleanliness for many people, you can skip washing dishes altogether on the last night of your trip. Instead, simply use the paper towels to clean the dirty dishes as much as possible and then wash them at home. Pack dirty dishes in airtight bags before putting them in your pack.

Dog and Horse Food

It's usually unwise to take dogs into bear country, and it's prohibited in most national parks. If you do it anyway, treat the dog food like human food. Store it in airtight bags, and hang it at night.

Although horses probably don't increase your risk of encountering a bear, the large amount of food necessary for horses can become a major bear attractant. Again, treat horse food as carefully as you do human food. Horse pellets are like candy bars to bears.

Safe Sex?

Although there is no real evidence to support this theory, some bear experts believe that human sexual activity attracts bears.

Camping above Timberline or Tree Line

Camping above timberline or north of the tree line makes food storage difficult, so avoid it when possible. If you must camp in alpine or tundra areas, use a BRFC and store it at least 200 yards downwind and downhill from your sleeping area at night.

If you don't have a BRFC, your remaining options are far from ideal. Keep all food and garbage in ziplock bags, and then double-bag them in large plastic bags. If you can find a cliff nearby, hang the double-bagged food over the cliff. If you can't find a cliff, put the bag on top of a large boulder to at least get it off the ground. One other option is to use a guaranteed waterproof bag and submerge food overnight.

One last option might be a portable electric fence, a fairly new innovation for backpackers. These fences can weigh less than four pounds, so if you know you'll be camping in a bear-dense area without good food-storage options, you might want to look at taking a portable electric fence.

Separating Fact from Hype

The Interagency Grizzly Bear Committee (IGBC) conducts a thorough testing program for many types of bear-resistant products such as BRFCs, electric fences, hanging devices, coolers, panniers, and garbage cans. Before you go shopping, check out the IGBC website (www.igbconline.org) for a list of approved products. Otherwise, you might buy something that isn't really bear resistant.

Vehicle Camping

Don't have the attitude that vehicle campgrounds offer added security from bears. In some cases, the reverse might be true.

If you're sleeping in a tent, there isn't much difference between backcountry camping and camping in a vehicle campground. Be equally careful with food and garbage.

One advantage you have in a vehicle campground is easier food storage. Except in a few national parks, where land managers discourage car storage because black bears have become adept at breaking into vehicles, keep food and garbage in airtight containers, and then stow them in your vehicle at night or when not in use. Keep all food smells out of the tent.

One disadvantage of vehicle campgrounds is the small size of the campsite. You can't effectively separate your sleeping area from your cooking area. When evaluating a vehicle campsite (no different than a backcountry site), look around for bear sign, and if you see any, go to another campground. If you see a culvert trap in the area, it usually means rangers are trying to remove problem bears, a good tip-off to go elsewhere.

Attractants and Repellents

Nobody really knows what attracts or repels bears, but everybody agrees on one thing: The smell of human food and garbage definitely attracts bears. If you don't want to attract bears, be extremely careful with food and garbage.

Bear experts also agree on two more things: Bears have a supersensitive sense of smell (seven times better than a bloodhound), and they're curious. Given these two facts, it seems best to avoid anything that might prompt a bear to investigate.

Try to blend into the natural environment instead of stand out from it. This means you should avoid things like brightly colored tents, backpacks, and clothing; camping in highly visible sites such as ridgelines or above timberline; making animal-like sounds; or using any kind of strong scent—all of which might excite a bear's curiosity.

Some recent research has indicated, for example, that bears might be attracted to bright colors, such as the yellow used in some backpacking tents and jackets, but ignore or barely notice dull, earth-tone colors, especially camouflage. At the same time, let's be realistic. There's no need, for example, to throw away your yellow tent, but instead, be careful not to display it prominently on a ridgeline where a bear can see it from a mile away. Don't present bears with a "visual cue" they simply can't ignore and, therefore, must approach to investigate.

Likewise, researchers have discovered that bears show interest in many strong scents, such as citronella (an ingredient in some insect repellents), fruity shampoos and lip balms, fuel for backpacking stoves, and human

THE BEAR ESSENTIALS:
Camping in Bear Country

Select a safe campsite.

Camp below timberline.

Separate cooking and sleeping areas.

Sleep in a tent.

Keep food odors out of the tent and packs.

Don't sleep in the same clothes used for cooking.

Cook the right amount of food and eat it all.

Store food and garbage out of the reach of bears.

Leave the campsite cleaner than you found it.

Immediately report any serious bear incident to rangers.

urine and feces. There needs to be more research, but in the meantime, it seems prudent to try to minimize the scents associated with being human. (And, of course, don't relieve yourself too close to camp.)

If scientists could come up with the right scent, sound, or color to keep bears out of our camps, there would be a collective sigh of relief, but until that happens, don't take chances. Avoid bright colors, unusual or loud sounds, and strong smells. Obviously, hikers and campers aren't using anything now that actively attracts bears; if they were, there would have been many more encounters.

Doing Somebody You Don't Know a Big Favor

Report all bear sightings to the ranger after your trip. This might not help you, but it could save another camper's life—and a bear's life, too. If rangers get enough reports to spot a pattern, they'll manage the area accordingly and not unknowingly allow camping in a potentially hazardous area.

For Your Protection

> *"Research clearly demonstrates that the normal response of grizzly bears is to avoid people and not to act aggressively or to attack, even if a person suddenly appears nearby."*
>
> —Stephen Herrero, *author of*
> Bear Attacks: Their Causes and Avoidance

The following sentence is the most important in this book. Protecting yourself from a bear is your second priority; your first priority is preventing a situation where you have to protect yourself. Nonetheless, if you have a close encounter with a bear and need protection, here are your options. If you round a corner in the trail and see a bear at close range, it may become necessary to protect yourself.

Gun-Shy?

Traditionally, travelers in bear country carried firearms, and in the hands of a skilled shooter, guns can offer the desired level of protection. Regrettably, the aftermath of this success is almost always a dead bear.

In unskilled hands, however, guns can make the situation worse. You need a heavy caliber, and a misplaced shot can wound and infuriate a bear. Gun handling experience is critical, and even the most skilled sharpshooter can easily get rattled and miss the target when it's a bear charging unexpectedly.

If you decide to carry a gun into the backcountry, which is now allowed in national parks, go to a gun expert and get good advice on what type of firearm to take. Then, before hitting the trail, practice, practice, practice.

Loud Noise

You can use guns as noisemakers to scare off bears. The same goes for loudly banging pans together, firecrackers, air horns, and any other loud noise. Loud noise might work better with black bears than with grizzlies.

Bear Pepper Spray

In recent years, bear pepper spray, which stings the eyes and hampers breathing, has earned more and more respect from experts. Many people have escaped unin- jured by using bear spray to turn away a charging bear. Now, most park rangers recommend it and carry it them- selves when in bear country.

In no recorded case has bear spray made a bear more aggressive or harmed the bear. In fact, getting sprayed might make a bear more wary of humans.

Even though bear spray can help erase that deep- seated fear that can ruin a wilderness adventure, it has a downside. Bear spray, like firearms, can create a false sense of security. Having bear spray mounted on your belt or pack strap doesn't mean you can skip the precautions outlined in this book.

Poor handling of food and garbage can get you (or other campers who follow you) into much more trouble than bear spray can solve. Canned pepper definitely does not make you bear-proof. Instead of being a cure-all, bear spray is merely your next-to-last line of defense. If it doesn't turn away the bear, your only remaining options are playing dead or physical resistance.

Here, point by point, are tips for using bear spray:

✔ Be sure you buy something called "Bear Spray" or "Bear Pepper Spray." Some products labeled "Pepper Spray" are not meant for use on bears.

✔ Before you leave the trailhead, read the directions on the bear spray container or packaging. If you're uncertain about how to operate the spray, buy an extra canister, test fire it, and discard it. Then, hit the trail with a new full canister. (You can also get inexpensive test canisters from some companies to familiarize yourself with operating the spray.)

✔ If you test-fire the canister, don't do it into the wind because it can drift back and give you the personal experience of what a bear feels like when sprayed.

✔ Don't test-fire bear spray in bear country, where the lingering smell might actually attract bears.

✔ Make sure you carry bear spray in an instantly accessible place. If you need it, you might only have one or two seconds to get ready to use it.

✔ All members of your party should carry bear spray at all times and keep it instantly accessible. Don't forget it when going into the woods for a nature call or leaving camp to go fishing or climbing.

✔ Keep bear spray close by when cooking. It won't do you much good 100 yards away in your pack if a bear, attracted by food smells, suddenly comes into camp.

✔ Don't spray it on yourself, your hiking partners, around camp, or on equipment. This might attract bears.

✔ Carry a large canister, 225 grams or more.

✔ Use a bear spray with a high level of active ingredient, 1 percent to 2 percent capsaicin.

✔ Make sure your bear spray is a fogger, not a stream pattern.

✔ Don't go for the lowest price; get a high-quality product.

✔ Remember the limited range of the spray, usually 20 to 30 feet.

✔ Don't let your bear spray get extremely cold or hot. Don't leave it in a hot vehicle all day. It could explode.

✔ Only use bear spray to deter charging or attacking bears, not on any other bear you see.

✔ Airlines prohibit taking bear spray on planes, so you might have to buy bear spray after you've reached your destination.

✔ In some cases, you might have trouble getting your bear spray across the U.S./Canada border, but recently Canada has started allowing travelers to cross with EPA-approved bear spray. Most major brands are EPA-approved.

THE BEAR ESSENTIALS:
Using Bear Spray

Attach your bear spray to your belt or
pack so it's instantly available. It won't
do any good if you can't be ready to
spray it in two seconds.

Draw your spray and remove the safety
clip immediately upon sighting a bear at
close range.

Don't attempt to spray unless the bear
approaches within 30 feet.

If the bear approaches within 30 feet,
give it a warning blast, placing a cloud of
spray between you and the bear.

If the bear continues to approach you
and gets within 20 feet, give it one or
two more blasts, aiming at the face.

If the bear approaches within 10 feet,
give it a five-second continuous blast,
aiming directly into the bear's face and
eyes. Continue to fire until the bear
retreats or the canister is empty.

Special Regulations for National Parks

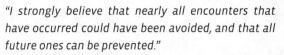

6

"I strongly believe that nearly all encounters that have occurred could have been avoided, and that all future ones can be prevented."

—Gary Brown, retired bear management specialist from Yellowstone National Park

It would be wonderful to have one checklist of things to do when venturing into bear country, but that's impossible. Bear populations vary their behavior, and black bears and grizzly bears often behave quite differently.

As a consequence, bear management specialists adjust regulations to match local conditions, especially in national parks. Carefully check regulations—for example, by scouring the park's website—preferably getting the information you need before leaving home.

This advance research allows you to acquire any special equipment you need, such as a BRFC, before getting to the entrance station and not being able to find what you need—or find it at a reasonable price. This preparation also saves time when you're anxious to hit the trail.

Many national parks require you to view a short video before getting a backcountry permit. This video, along with handouts, explains specific regulations for the park.

In a few cases, recommendations in this book, such as information on food storage, party size, noisemaking methods, or your reaction to an encounter, might not be totally in line with local regulations and recommendations, which should take precedence over advice offered here or in any other book. For example, some parks have experienced heavy recreational use and have bear populations that have learned to retrieve food sacks hung in trees. These parks have developed alternative bear-resistant devices, such as metal hanging poles or large steel storage lockers installed at designated campsites. Other parks require you to carry your food in BRFCs. Another major difference is dog regulations. You can take your dog into most public lands, but most national parks prohibit dogs on backcountry trails.

Bear Jams

National parks can be a great place to safely view bears from a roadway, but when a bear shows itself near a park roadway, watch out. Everybody stops to see it, and presto, the park has a "bear jam."

Bear jams can be chaotic situations with people doing stupid things, so be careful. Don't have a false sense of security because you're near your vehicle. Here are some tips on keeping yourself and bears safe.

- If traffic is heavy, slow down or stop and be patient.

- If traffic is light, pull off the road only if there is a pullout or other safe stop. Don't stop in the middle of the road—and watch for other drivers who might not follow this advice.

- Watch other vehicles and pedestrians who might be concentrating on the bear and making erratic movements, such as crossing the road in front of you without checking for traffic.

- If you stop, don't take too much time. Traffic is backing up behind you, and you should give others a chance to see the bear.

- Stay in your vehicle.

- Never approach the bear for a better photo or for any other reason.

- Never try to lure the bear closer for a photograph.

- Never feed bears.

- If a ranger is on duty there, follow his or her directions immediately.

- If you see a No Stopping sign, follow this advice. Rangers may be trying to change bear behavior by avoiding bear jams. Give the bear a better chance of surviving by not stopping and triggering a bear jam.

Visitors to national parks can unintentionally be responsible for the death of roadside bears. Bears that become semi-tame or stressed by people getting too close may react aggressively and cause an injury. Then, in many cases, rangers have little choice but to kill the bear.

Alaska National Parks

Alaska has more bears than the rest of the United States. The state also has many national parks and other areas managed by the National Park Service (NPS), all with different regulations. This makes it vitally important to check park-specific regulations before traveling to Alaska to hike in any of these bear-rich parks. For example, Alaskan national parks still recommend different reactions with brown/grizzly bears than with black bears. In Alaska, the NPS recommends always fighting back instead of playing dead in any black bear encounter. "Never play dead with a black bear," the Alaskan national park brochure firmly states. "Most black bear attacks are predatory."

Denali National Park requires backpackers to use BRFCs in some areas and recommends them in all areas of the park. You can rent one for free from the park.

Katmai National Park also requires BRFCs when backpacking and has a limited supply for free rental. Katmai sets up electric fences around frontcountry campsites and recommends backpackers use their own electric fence in the backcountry. The park also wants anglers to stop fishing if a bear moves into the same area; break off a hooked fish (by cutting the line or jerking the hook out of the fish's mouth), and then move to a new fishing spot.

Banff, Jasper, and Other Canadian National Parks

Bear experts from Canadian national parks reviewed the information in this book and said it fits the general bear management and advice they distribute. They recommend being particularly cautious and not having a false sense of security while viewing bears from a road. Some Canadian national parks require BRFCs.

In 2011, for the first time in any national park, Parks Canada mandated that until September 15 hikers on the popular Lake Minnewanka Trail in Banff National Park must travel in a tight group of four or more, and at least one member of the group must carry bear pepper spray at all times.

Glacier National Park

Bear management experts in Glacier recommend using loud human voices or loud clapping of hands instead of metallic noise when hiking backcountry trails.

Great Smoky Mountains National Park

Great Smoky Mountains has a healthy population of black bears, but no grizzly bears, and unlike Western black bear populations—which also display various phases of brown—all black bears in Great Smoky Mountains are black. Bear management experts at Great Smoky Mountains do not recommend trying to burn leftovers or garbage, even if campfires are permitted, because the park believes this can lead to "nuisance bear activity."

The park also recommends using physical resistance in all encounters, keeping in mind that an "encounter" is defined as a situation where you might be at risk, not simply a situation in which you see a bear. In case of an encounter, yell and throw rocks; band together with your companions to seem larger and more threatening; move to higher ground; and do whatever else you can to intimidate and scare the bear. Don't turn away or run from the bear. Don't let the bear get food unless you have to abandon it to protect yourself. In case of physical contact, fight back. Don't play dead.

Grand Teton National Park

Regulations in Grand Teton National Park match most of the other parks in this book, with the exception of food storage. Many campsites in Grand Teton have community metal food lockers, and hikers are required to use them for food storage. In lesser-used areas with no food lockers, the park requires the use of BRFCs.

Yosemite National Park

Park regulations require backpackers and campers to use BRFCs in most areas. A few designated campsites have metal food lockers or "bear boxes," but even when using these campsites, the NPS recommends carrying food in BRFCs, and Yosemite's website includes a list of places to buy or rent approved BRFCs.

Along with food and garbage, the park requires back-packers to store other scented items, such as sunscreen and toothpaste, in food lockers or BRFCs. The park also recommends storing garbage in the portable canisters and packing it out instead of trying to burn it.

The park, in essence, wants hikers to never leave food or garbage unattended, even momentarily, for example, when going to the lake for a swim or taking a nap. Always keep food and garbage in food lockers or BRFCs, except when eating or preparing meals.

In vehicle campgrounds in Yosemite's frontcountry areas, the park requires you to store food and all other scented items in food lockers provided at all camp-grounds. Don't store food or scented items in vehicles, and never leave food in a vehicle overnight. If you don't need it or don't have room in the food locker, throw it away in a bear-resistant garbage container.

Sequoia and Kings Canyon National Parks

In these parks, the NPS requires BRFCs in some areas and recommends use in all areas—for food, garbage, and all other scented items. Some backcountry campsites also have metal food lockers.

Special Precautions for Women

7

The risk is minimal and acceptable. We all accept some element of risk in our daily life. That risk is not appreciably higher in bear country.
— Stephen Herrero, *author of* Bear Attacks: Their Causes and Avoidance

Most bear-country hiking and camping techniques apply equally to men and women; however, women should take a few extra precautions.

The Best Smell: No Smell

As recommended earlier in this book, you should avoid strong smells when in bear country. This goes for men and women. Many feminine products, such as shampoo, soap, and lotion, tend to be more heavily scented. In addition to not using these strong-smelling products on the trail, refrain from using them at home the day before you plan to enter bear country. Search for unscented products, or even better, go without. You do not need cosmetics or perfume in the wilderness.

Menstruation

For decades, bear experts have disagreed on the safety of women traveling in bear country during their menstrual periods. Some authorities recommend that women stay out of bear country during menstrual periods, but others consider this an overreaction.

Field tests under controlled conditions have shown that bears are attracted to menstrual odor and several other strong odors. To date, however, scientists have found no evidence that bears are attracted to menstrual odor more than any other strong odor. In addition, no known bear attack has been traced to menstruation as a cause. Nonetheless, common sense dictates that since bears have a keen sense of smell, women should take extra precautions.

Keep yourself as clean and odor-free as possible.

Use premoistened, unscented cleaning towelettes, and use tampons instead of pads.

Never bury used tampons or towelettes in the backcountry. A bear could easily smell them and dig up this little "reward." This could endanger the next person coming down the trail.

Place all used tampons and towelettes in double ziplock bags, and store them with other garbage in a metal food storage locker or BRFC or hang them 10 feet off the ground.

Making the Choice

No scientific evidence exists to indicate women are at greater risk during menstrual periods than at any other time. If you choose to go into bear country, take all special precautions as outlined above and elsewhere in this book, and enjoy the trip.

Special Precautions for Hunters, Anglers, and Outfitters

"Simply put, the great bear has all the strikes against recovery that the creator could have bestowed upon it, including finding its last refuge in the well-armed West that looks to John Wayne for a role model. It is still true today that very few bears die of natural death; almost all die because we kill them."

—Louisa Willcox, senior wildlife advocate for the Natural Resources Defense Council

This book outlines the steps you can take to make your trip to bear country as safe as possible, but if you wanted to make the trip as hazardous as possible, you would employ many techniques commonly used by hunters and anglers. Hunters want to surprise wildlife, and they work hard at being as quiet as possible. The same goes for anglers stalking a big trout in a mountain stream. Consequently, hunters and anglers must make a difficult compromise between safety and success.

For Hunters and Outfitters

Hunters (especially big-game hunters) commonly sneak silently through the woods during early morning and late evening or quietly stalk through bear country in darkness to reach a vantage point or stand before first light—in camouflaged clothing laced with buck scent or elk urine. Such behavior is diametrically opposite of all recommendations in this book. Worse, perhaps, some bear experts believe bears might be attracted by gunfire by associating it with the presence of fresh meat or a gut pile.

No wonder so many encounters between hunters and bears occur every year during fall hunting seasons.

Even though there's a limit to what hunters can do to prevent bear encounters and still hope for any chance of a successful hunt, they should consider these extra precautions:

- When hiking to a favorite spot during darkness, use a flashlight.

- When camping out, select and set up a safe camp as outlined in the Camping in Bear Country chapter.

- Don't hunt alone.

- Make extra noise when driving game out of thick brush or dense thickets of small trees.

- If you see a carcass or gut pile left by another hunter, don't go near it.

- If a big-game hunt is successful, field-dress the animal and get it out of the backcountry as quickly as possible.

- Rapidly separate the carcass from the gut pile. Use a sheet of heavy plastic to move the gut pile about 100 yards from the carcass.

- Don't leave your gut pile near a trail or campsite where a bear might claim it and create circumstances that could threaten other hunters or hikers using the trail or campsite.

- Don't drag a carcass into camp. A bear might follow the scent trail.

- If you leave a carcass unattended, hang it 10 feet off the ground, which is required in some national forests. If necessary, cut the meat into smaller pieces to facilitate hanging.

- Hang any carcasses at least 100 yards from any campsite or trail as required in some national forests. If it isn't possible to hang the carcass, cache it at least 100 yards from camp.

- If you can't hang the carcass, leave it on the ground in an open area where you can observe it from a safe distance when you return to claim your prize.

- Leave an article of clothing (ripe with human scent) on or near the carcass or pour ammonia around the carcass to deter bears.

- Noisily return to the carcass upwind, so the bear can get your scent before you get there. Thoroughly scan the area with binoculars before approaching the carcass. If you see that the carcass has been moved or partially buried, a bear may have claimed it. If a bear claims the carcass, abandon it and leave the area immediately.

- Don't attempt to shoot or harass the bear that has claimed your carcass.

- Use horses to decrease the chance of a bear encounter.

- Watch for signs of bear activity and know bear habitat.

- When bugling for elk, be alert. Bugling not only attracts elk, but in a few cases, bears, too.

For Anglers

Anglers can also make their trip safer with a few extra precautions:

- Don't fish alone.

- Remember that bears like to travel along streams and lakeshores, so when following a loud, rushing mountain stream in thick brush, make lots of noise.

- Catch-and-release fishing is much less likely to attract a bear than is having fish for dinner. Seriously consider not keeping and eating fish in bear country, particularly when you can't have a hot campfire to burn entrails and leftovers.

- Don't bury fish entrails. Instead, burn them or pack them out. When fishing in large streams or deep lakes, you can clean the fish right where you catch them (instead of back at camp) and, after puncturing the air bladder, throw entrails into the deep water. Never leave entrails along lakeshores or in small streams.

- If you want fish for dinner, keep those you catch in the water as long as possible to keep the smell to a minimum.

- Don't clean fish within 200 yards of camp.

- Avoid getting fish odors on your clothes, and wash hands thoroughly after cleaning fish.

Special Precautions for Mountain Bikers

"Only those able to see the pageant of evolution can be expected to value its theater, the wilderness, or its outstanding achievement, the grizzly."
　　　　　—Aldo Leopold, author and conservationist

Mountain bikers should, of course, carefully follow all precautions for hikers, but they can take a few extra steps to make their trip even safer.

Noise Is Even More Important

Mountain bikers coasting a steep hill can build up speed and, in most cases, don't make much noise, both of which combine to create a hazardous situation. The speed and relative silence of biking probably won't alert a bear around a blind corner or over a small hill, and this potentially could cause a sudden encounter. Cranking up a long hill isn't without potential danger either; don't forget to look around for bears and make noise.

Human voices probably won't be loud enough, so rely on metallic noise. Attach a bear bell to your saddle or handlebar. The bell will constantly clang as you ride down a bumpy trail. Distracting? Yes, but safety first. You can also buy hand-operated handlebar bells to ring whenever visibility is impaired, such as on a long descent with blind curves.

Moonlight bike rides are increasing in popularity, but they increase your chances of an encounter. Don't ride at night in bear country.

Special Precautions for Photographers

"We should preserve grizzly bear populations, not because their ecological function is critical, but because of what they can do for human imagination, thought and experience."

—Stephen Herrero, author of
Bear Attacks: Their Causes and Avoidance

Trying to get a good photo of a bear, especially of a grizzly, is always risky, and photographers have been mauled and killed in failed attempts to do so. Nonetheless, photographers, it seems, find it difficult to pass up the chance to get a good bear photo.

- Use at least a telephoto lens.

- Avoid direct eye contact with a bear, which it could interpret as an act of aggression.

- Don't make unusual sounds or throw things to prompt a bear into a better pose.

- If the bear moves away, don't follow it.

- Maintain a distance of 1,000 feet or more, but remember that under some circumstances, this can still be dangerous.

- Immediately, slowly, and carefully retreat at any sign of a bear becoming aggressive, but don't panic and run.

- Be particularly cautious when photographing a female with cubs.

- Set up near an escape tree tall enough to get 15 feet off the ground.

- Never approach or try to sneak up on a bear.

- Never feed or leave food in an attempt to attract a bear. This is not only unethical but also dangerous for you and for other people coming into the area later.

It bears repeating: Don't be tempted to get too close to bears when trying to photograph them. More than one would-be photographer has encountered serious trouble by getting too close.

Close Encounters

11

"The thing that makes me very unhappy about the whole incident is my fear that this will only add fuel to the fire for those people who advocate the destruction of the grizzly to make our national parks safe. There is no reason, in the name of civilized progress, to kill an animal for doing what is natural. I feel no malice toward the bear. It was my fault for sticking my neck out too far. The bear was only protecting her young and her territory. The only thing that will prevent me from hiking in the wilderness again is the eventual destruction of the wilderness itself, and when anyone advocates the destruction of grizzlies, he is in essence advocating the destruction of the true wilderness. Let us pray that this never happens."

—*Robert Hahm, mauling victim*

The threat of having a close encounter with a bear is like the threat of having a heart attack. If you practice preventive health care, stay physically fit, and watch your diet, you're much less likely to have heart problems. Likewise, if you follow the safety guidelines in this book, you're much less likely to have a close encounter with a bear. With both heart attacks and bear attacks, preventing a problem is so much better than dealing with the problem.

Defining an Encounter

In this book, a bear sighting (seeing a bear at a safe distance) is not considered an encounter. An encounter is a situation where you may be at risk. An encounter could be surprising a bear at close range on or off the trail, a bear slowly or rapidly approaching you, a bear coming into camp, or a predatory attack. An encounter becomes an attack if a bear makes physical contact with you.

No Consensus

If you're uncertain about what to do in case of an encounter, you aren't alone. Even bear experts disagree on how to react to various kinds of encounters.

Every encounter is different, every person is different, and every bear is different. Consequently, there's no checklist for what to do. Nonetheless, your reaction to an encounter can definitely affect your chances of coming away uninjured.

Defensive or Offensive?

The most recent recommendations from bear scientists and managers divide all encounters into two categories—defensive and offensive. Defensive encounters are situations where you startle a bear, and the bear could be as surprised as you are. In defensive encounters, you have accidentally broken into the defensive perimeter or violated the personal space of a bear and suddenly pose a threat to the bear, its cubs, or its food cache.

Offensive—or as bear experts prefer to say, "non-defensive"—encounters involve aggressive or predatory bears that intentionally move toward you. Most likely, but not always, the non-defensive bear is bluffing or simply curious instead of truly aggressive or predatory.

Previously, bear managers had different recommendations for black bears and grizzly bears, but now, in most cases, they lump all bears together and split them up as defensive or non-defensive bears, and it's important to understand and recognize the difference because this dictates what you do. In other words, note the behavior, not the species.

The Rehearsal

Not many recommendations apply to all encounters, but one does: Cool heads prevail. Panic is your greatest enemy. To help avoid panic, do rehearsals before you hit the trail. Go through hypothetical situations and decide what each member of the group should do. This rehearsal builds self-confidence.

Playing Dead

Bear experts used to recommend playing dead by curling up in the cannonball position, but most now recommend lying flat on your stomach, legs slightly separated, hands clasped behind your neck, elbows extended. This position gives your vital organs as much protection as possible and makes it hard for the bear to turn you over. It also protects your face area that bears commonly attack.

While playing dead, remain silent and leave your pack on to provide extra protection. If the bear turns you over, continue rolling back onto your stomach. Remain playing dead until you're sure the bear has left the area.

If You See a Bear at a Distance

First and most important, don't move toward the bear while you enjoy this rare and beautiful sight.

If the bear is a long distance from the trail, enjoy the sight and continue down the trail. If the bear is uncomfortably close to the trail ahead but is acting naturally and not moving toward you, slowly back down the trail about a quarter-mile, keeping an eye on the bear until out of sight.

Wait a few minutes and then hike back up the trail making lots of loud noise. If the bear is still near the trail ahead and still acting naturally, take a big detour around the bear, upwind if possible, so the bear can get your scent. Stay out of sight, if possible, and make lots of noise to ensure the bear knows you're there. Then, quickly (walk, don't run) leave the area.

If You Suddenly See a Bear at Close Range

Most important, don't panic or run wildly or scream. Running or other rapid movements might cause the bear to charge. As long as you stay cool-headed and under control, you have an excellent chance of leaving a sudden encounter with only vivid memories, not injuries. If you act like prey, you can become prey.

The first thing to do is nothing. Stand still. Be quiet. Slowly take your bear spray from its holster and remove the safety clip. Keep your backpack on. Look around for cubs. Then, carefully assess the situation. Ask yourself: Is this a defensive or non-defensive bear?

Watch for aggressive behavior, such as laid-back ears, hackles up on the back of its neck, head rapidly swinging from side to side, threatening "woofs," or feet slapping on the ground. If the bear mashes its teeth together making a loud "pop," it's very agitated and likely to charge. If the bear stands on its hind feet and puts its snout up, it isn't a sign of aggression. The bear is trying to get your scent or get a better look to figure out what you are.

If you decide to climb a tree, make sure you have time to reach the tree and get 15 feet up it before the bear can get there. Running toward the tree could easily prompt the bear to chase you. Remember, bears can sprint at up to 35 miles per hour. In several documented encounters, people have underestimated a bear's speed and been mauled as they tried to reach or climb a tree.

Any bear that intentionally moves toward you should be considered non-defensive. It might just be curious, but could also be at least aggressive and possibly predatory. This or any other aggressive behavior is your cue that the bear wants you out of its turf, so back away slowly, talking quietly in a monotone. Avoid rapid movements. Don't turn your back on the bear; instead, turn sideways to the bear if you can. Be non-threatening and submissive. Avoid direct eye contact with the bear. As you slowly retreat, slowly move your arms up and down—like doing jumping jacks without jumping. You can drop something on the trail (clothing, walking stick, etc.) to distract the bear, but not anything with food in it. You don't want to give the bear a food reward for chasing you.

If the bear continues to follow you, stop. Stand your ground. If the bear also stops, try again to slowly back away. If the bear charges and it looks like physical contact is imminent, use your bear spray or firearm.

If a Bear Continues to Approach You

When facing a non-defensive bear, it's important to stand your ground. An initially curious or mildly aggressive bear could become predatory if you don't stand up to it.

At first, stand still, remain calm, and talk in a monotone voice. Slowly move out of the bear's path. It may just want the trail, so give it up. If the bear continues to follow you off the trail, it's probably an aggressive or predatory bear, so stop and stand your ground. Challenge the bear with eye contact and a louder, firmer voice. Act aggressively to tell the bear you plan to fight. The longer the bear continues to approach, the more aggressive you should be. Shout at the bear. Make other loud noises. Keep your group close together to look bigger and more threatening. Try to get higher than the bear by going to higher ground or standing on rocks or logs. If none of this prompts the bear to retreat and the bear comes within range, use your bear spray or firearm.

If a Bear Charges You

It's easy to say and hard to do, but again, don't panic. Most charges are bluffs and stop short of physical contact. Point your bear spray or firearm at the bear and stand your ground. Sometimes a bear will make several bluff charges. Don't spray or shoot the bear unless you're sure the bear isn't bluffing and likely to make contact—and is within range, i.e., less than 30 feet for bear spray. If the bear stops after a bluff charge, slowly wave your arms, talk softly, and slowly back away. Again, you can drop something without food in it to distract the bear. If the bear doesn't stop, use your spray or gun.

If a Bear Makes Physical Contact

If a bear charges and makes physical contact with you, it's important to quickly decide whether the attack is defensive or non-defensive. If you surprised the bear and it charged you suddenly out of nowhere, it's probably a defensive attack by a bear threatened by your unexpectedly appearing nearby—or it might be defending its cubs or food cache. Act submissive and play dead.

Even if a defensive bear roughs you up, don't fight back. Remain flat on your stomach and silent. Don't look at the bear. If the bear moves away, be patient and continue playing dead until you're sure it has left the area. Then, immediately (no running!) move out of the area.

In most defensive attacks, the bear will retreat when it's sure you no longer pose a threat, but if the bear continues the attack and becomes predatory, fight back anyway you can.

If you know the bear has purposely moved toward you, getting closer and closer until it has made physical contact with you, consider it an aggressive or predatory bear. In such an attack, don't play dead or act submissive. If you can't escape up a tree or into a vehicle or building, fight back with all your might and with whatever weapons you can find. Concentrate your defense on the head, nose and eyes of the bear.

It might seem futile to face an opponent many times faster and stronger than you are, but you might be surprised what you can do in a life-threatening situation. If you see one of your companions in this situation, intervene on his or her behalf.

If You See a Bear from Camp

If the bear is a long way from camp, get your bear spray out and make lots of noise to scare it away. If there's still time before nightfall, break camp and move to another campsite. Seeing a bear circling a camp during the day might mean it has become food conditioned or is at least habituated to human activity and could come into camp, perhaps at night.

If the bear is close to camp, move to the base of the escape tree you previously scouted out. Take noisemakers and bear spray with you. If the bear comes closer, climb the tree. Take the food with you, if possible, so the bear doesn't get a food reward.

If you don't have a good escape tree or time to climb it, stand together to look bigger and more threatening to the bear; everyone should have bear spray ready to fire. Shout and act aggressively. If the bear comes dangerously close, spray it—or if you chose to also carry a firearm, use it.

If a Bear Comes into Camp during Daylight

A bear coming into camp is not the same type of bear that you surprise on the trail. This bear has chosen to approach you and is definitely a non-defensive bear.

It could be a bear that has become conditioned to human food and garbage, possibly by people who camped there before you. This bear is more dangerous because it has stopped trying to avoid an encounter. The bear might not intend to attack. More likely, it's only looking for another food reward. Try to prevent the bear from getting it. Allowing the bear to get more food only makes it more dangerous for you and the next campers.

Stay calm. Avoid direct eye contact. Stay together in a close group to look bigger and more threatening. Talk softly, and slowly retreat. If you have to abandon the camp and sacrifice your camping gear, do it. Return to the trailhead and immediately report the encounter to a ranger.

If the bear moves toward you, react in the same way you would if it approached you on the trail.

If a Bear Comes into Camp at Night

First, make sure it's a bear instead of a campground deer or one of your hiking partners answering a nature call. Get the bear spray or firearm ready to fire and use your flashlight to verify that it's a bear.

If it's a bear and you have time to get to your escape tree, do it, but don't leave the tent if you aren't sure you have time to get up the tree. If the bear is hanging around the cooking area because of the food smell, make lots of noise and try to scare the bear away.

If a Bear Enters Your Tent

This is the worst possible situation, but fortunately, it very rarely happens.

A night attack comes from a predatory bear. Don't act like prey. Don't lie still in your sleeping bag. Don't play dead. Don't run or scream, but don't be passive either. If you can't escape to a vehicle or building or up a tree, fight back with everything you have. Use the bear spray. Make loud noise. Shine your flashlight in the bear's eyes. Temporarily blind the bear with the flash on your camera. Whack it on the nose with your flashlight or walking stick. Use whatever physical resistance you can.

Generalizations as Dangerous as Bears

The above suggestions have been boiled down from personal experience, extensive research of written literature, and many discussions with bear experts. But these are still only general guidelines. They won't work every time with every bear. Special situations and special bears won't fit guidelines.

One thing is clear: Stay calm and try to rationally evaluate the situation to determine what type of bear you face. If you have studied up on bears and if your group has had a rehearsal, you can, in most cases, safely survive an encounter.

Be Realistic

After reading a few pages about how to deal with encounters, it might be harder to overcome the fear of bears, but be realistic. If you practice the methods outlined in this book and given to you at the local ranger station, it's extremely unlikely that you'll ever have a close encounter with a bear. And even if you do, you have an excellent chance of coming away uninjured.

If bears wanted to prey on humans, it would be easy for them. Bears could easily kill hundreds of people per year, but then, of course, there wouldn't be any bears because we would kill them all. Obviously, 99-plus percent want to avoid people. Keep this in mind as you prepare for—and then enjoy—your trip to bear country.

THE BEAR ESSENTIALS:
Surviving an Encounter or Attack

For all encounters . . .

- Every encounter is different.

- Preventing the encounter is the highest priority.

- Have a rehearsal.

- Carry bear spray and know how to use it.

- Cool heads prevail; panic is your greatest enemy.

- If you act like prey, you become prey. Never run unless you're positive you can reach safety before the bear can.

- Determine whether it's a defensive or nondefensive bear.

- Any bear coming into camp is dangerous.

- A night attack comes from a predatory bear.

- Keep the risk of an attack in perspective; they're extremely rare.

- Report all encounters.

THE BEAR ESSENTIALS:
Surviving an Encounter or Attack
(continued)

If approached by a defensive bear . . .

- Act submissive and nonthreatening, talk in a calm voice, and get your bear spray ready to fire.

- If the bear stops, slowly back away.

- If the bear continues to come closer, stand your ground and talk softly.

- If the bear comes very close and contact is likely, use your bear spray.

- If the bear spray doesn't work, play dead.

- If the bear stops its attack, continue playing dead until you're sure it has left the area.

- If the bear continues its attack, stop playing dead and aggressively fight back and intervene to help others in the same situation.

If approached by an aggressive or predatory bear . . .

- Get your bear spray or firearm ready to fire.

- Slowly move out of the bear's path and talk softly.

- If the bear follows you, stop and stand your ground.

- If you have people with you, stand closely together to look bigger and more threatening.

- Act aggressively, shout and make other loud noises, and make yourself and your party look as big and as threatening as possible.

- If the bear comes very close, spray it, or if you have a firearm, use it.

- If the bear makes physical contact, don't play dead. Fight as hard as you can, concentrating on the head, nose, and eyes.

Quick review . . .

- With defensive bears, act submissive and play dead.

- With aggressive or predatory bears, act threatening and fight back.

Living or Vacationing in Bear Country

12

"Keeping bears wild keeps them alive. Kindness kills wildness."

—Parks Canada

More and more people are moving into bear country or at least spending a week or two there on a summer vacation. Hardly a day goes by without news of a new resort or mine, most with accompanying residential developments. Second homes and wilderness cabins continue to sprout in many privately owned meadows in bear country. In short, more and more people are living in bear country with more and more chance of conflict with bears. If bears, and particularly grizzly bears, are to survive this forced coexistence, the residents of bear country must consider the impact their daily activities has on bears, as well as their own safety.

Garbage Bears

Your garbage could kill somebody.

A "garbage bear" is a soon-to-be-dead bear, and somebody might get hurt along the way. If you live in or visit bear country, you must be extremely careful not to let bears get human food or garbage. You don't want to be responsible for a regrettable chain of events that could kill somebody—and most likely will kill a bear.

Garbage is like bear candy, or more appropriate, like bear drugs, and in many places, still an uncontrolled substance. It might be useless waste to us, but to bears garbage has extremely high nutritional value. It only takes one garbage meal for a bear to get hooked. The bear becomes conditioned to garbage and will go to extremes to get it. The bear will return again and again looking for more garbage. If it can't get a food reward at your place, it will go to your neighbor's place. The bear might even abandon its normal wariness of humankind and come dangerously close to people to get food or garbage. It will climb over fences, break into cabins, or rip open dumpsters and vehicles.

Sooner or later, a fed bear is a dead bear. But before the bear is killed, it might injure a child playing in a backyard or a hiker on a nearby trail. If it can't get human food from cabins, it might try getting some out of a backpacker's tent.

Everybody living in bear country bears the responsibility of keeping garbage away from bears. It goes with the territory.

Storing Garbage

If you use outside garbage cans, don't put food items into them. Use outside garbage cans for non-food items only. Better yet, keep garbage in the barn, garage, or basement, completely unavailable to bears. Try to store it in a manner that prevents odors from escaping.

Many communities and most national parks have bear-proof dumpsters, incinerators, or other approved disposal facilities. If you decide to live in bear country, take the extra time needed to haul your garbage to these facilities. You can also buy bear-resistant garbage containers for your house.

Watch the Kids

Closely supervise children. They're little and helpless and might look like easy prey to bears (even more so to mountain lions). Don't allow kids to hike out of sight without adult supervision. You might be super-conscious about not creating bear–human conflicts, but do you know what your neighbors have been doing? Even if you haven't had bears visiting your place, a garbage bear could still be lurking nearby.

Pets and Livestock

Use the same level of caution for pet and livestock food as you do for human food and garbage. Bears love horse pellets and dog food. Don't let them get it. When you feed livestock, try not to spill pellets, oats, or other food on the ground.

Honey Bears

No surprise. Bears love honey. They also love the larval form of bees. If you live in bear country and have beehives, you'll probably have bear problems. Make the hives inaccessible to bears. One common method is putting the hives on platforms at least 10 feet off the ground. Use metal poles or cover the wooden support poles with tin to prevent bears from climbing up for their honey treat. You can also use electric fencing to fend off bears.

Fruits and Vegetables

Fruit trees and vegetable gardens attract bears like magnets, and it's almost impossible to keep them away, especially during years when natural foods have a bad crop. If you live in bear country, you really should not plant fruit trees. In addition to creating a hazardous situation for you, your family, and your neighbors, bears that become overly bold in raiding fruit trees are usually killed.

THE BEAR ESSENTIALS:
Living or Vacationing
in Bear Country

Never, never, never feed bears.

Make sure bears never get human food or garbage.

Keep food odors to a minimum.

Keep bird, pet, and livestock food away from bears.

Keep compost piles in enclosed buildings.

Put electric fencing around beehives, fruit trees, and vegetable gardens.

Talk to neighbors about proper handling of garbage and other bear attractants.

Closely supervise children.

If you have fruit trees, the best defense against bears is electric fencing. Also, try to pick all the fruit immediately after it ripens to cut down the amount of time it tempts bears. Ditto for vegetable gardens.

Compost
Many residents of remote areas like to use composting to cut down the amount of refuse they create. That's generally sound environmental practice, but in bear country, the odor of decomposing food in compost heaps can attract bears. If you live in bear country, you should not compost refuse. If you must compost, do it in an enclosed area like a garage or barn.

Bird Feeders or Bear Feeders?
Bird feeders, particularly if you use suet, attract bears. Only use suet in winter months when bears are busy sleeping under a snowbank. Hang hummingbird feeders out of reach of bears. Take platform feeders in at night or put them on long, metal poles out of reach of bears.

Risk Factors
Many people think staying close to residential communities is safer than hiking deep into the wilderness. The reverse may be true.

More people always means more garbage, and if somebody hasn't used proper disposal, there could be a dangerous bear hanging around a developed area. Conversely, most hikers nowadays use zero-impact camping techniques and are very careful not to let bears get human food or garbage. A remote campsite could be safer than a backyard picnic.

Working in Bear Country

13

"North America–wide, tens of thousands of bears are killed each year because of conflicts with humans. In British Columbia alone, an average of 824 black bears and 48 grizzlies are shot by conservation officers every year because they are considered a 'problem.' These preventable human-bear conflicts also result in human injury and, very occasionally, death, as well as thousands of dollars in property damage. The good news is these very negative consequences can be avoided by bear-proofing your campsite, home, workplace, neighborhood and community."

—Get Bear Smart Society

Working in bear country does not differ significantly from playing in bear country. In both cases, think bear. Ironically, in some cases, people visiting bear country for a few days tend to be more careful and knowledgeable than people who work there and become nonchalant and careless. But the principles of bear awareness apply to all who enter bear country, for work or play.

Employer Responsibility

Companies hiring people to work in bear country should consider bears along with other safety issues and make sure employees are well trained and informed. Employers should provide basic bear awareness training and provide reading material.

Stress internal communications about safety issues, including bears. Keep records of bear sign and sightings and share this information with others working in the area. If possible, use radios, cell phones, or satellite phones for instant communication. Have workers travel in pairs. Make sure there's a plan for meticulous handling of food and garbage, even field lunches, so bears don't get food rewards from workers. All workers should carry bear pepper spray and be trained on how to use it.

Remote Camps

Consult with local wildlife officials before picking a location for a remote base camp, and set it up with bears in mind. Avoid locating camps in natural bear travel or feeding areas. Similar to backpacking campsites, separate the sleeping and cooking areas and keep all food odors out of the sleeping area.

Most bear incidents in remote camps involve poor handling of bear attractants, most notably garbage, which should be immediately incinerated or hauled out of the backcountry—and never buried. Large camps often must deal with more attractants than the universal problem of food and garbage, such as sewage, gray water, petroleum products, cooking grease, and any other strong-smelling by-product of a long-term camp. Consult local health authorities on how best to treat and handle these attractants to keep them from attracting bears.

Deterrents

In addition to providing bear spray for each employee, large camps should have other bear deterrents normally used by bear managers. Consult with local wildlife officials on the most appropriate deterrents, such as air horns

THE BEAR ESSENTIALS:
Working in Bear Country

Include bear awareness in any field safety plan.

Make sure bears never get human food or garbage.

Work in pairs if possible.

Carry bear pepper spray and know how to use it.

Carefully handle all attractants in camps.

Have bear deterrents and be trained in their use.

Install bear detection devices.

Have at least one firearm capable of killing a bear in camp.

Have a response plan for a bear coming into camp.

and other noisemakers, explosive devices, and cracker shells and nonlethal projectiles (rubber slugs or bean bags) fired from 12-gauge shotguns, All personnel likely to be in a position to use these deterrents should be properly trained in their use.

Installing an electric fence around camp is also an excellent bear deterrent.

Bear-Detection Devices

Large camps should consider bear-detection devices such as trip wires or infrared beams around the perimeter of camp. Also, a well-trained dog with a good handler can help alert people in camp of an approaching bear.

Firearms

All camps should have at least one firearm capable of killing a bear, such as a large-caliber hunting rifle or shotgun loaded with rifled slugs or double-ought buckshot, but it should only be used as a last resort and in defense of life and property. Working hard at not attracting bears into camp is the first priority—and much easier on the bear.

Helicopters or Airplanes

Some companies use helicopters or small planes to transport employees to remote locations. Before landing, the pilot should circle the area looking for bears. Also, when transporting bear spray, pack it in airtight containers, preferably in the baggage compartment. An accidental discharge could disable the pilot.

Afterword: Thinking Grizzly

"In a deeply tribal sense, we love our monsters."
—E. O. Wilson, biologist, conservationist, and author

This book offers tips for protecting yourself from all bears, not only grizzly bears, but in reality, many readers tend to be most concerned about grizzlies. That's why I'm devoting this afterword to a few personal opinions about the mightiest bear of them all, the grizzly.

Something happens to people who see a grizzly in a wild setting. It changes them. It brings a tear of joy to their eyes. It leaves an everlasting mark on their psyche. I would, in fact, argue that it's the best thing you can see, period. Viewing a grizzly in a zoo might be enjoyable and help with identification and build some appreciation for threatened wildlife, but it's a far cry from watching a female grizzly shepherd her cubs across a mountain meadow.

I'm a lucky guy. I spend several weeks every year in grizzly country, and I've seen lots of wild grizzlies in spectacular settings. I also spend countless hours reliving those magnificent moments.

I've taken my children into the heart of the wilderness with the specific goal of seeing a grizzly. They've seen several, and I'm positive those experiences are permanently etched into their memories.

Now, my children have grown and gone out to see grizzlies on their own. Today they're taking their own children out to see a wild grizzly.

For me, it can't get any better than that.

In more than forty years of hiking, mostly in grizzly country, I have had one serious encounter and a few sightings that were close enough to get my adrenaline flowing. I'll remember every detail of these experiences until the day I die.

But there is a problem with such thinking. As more and more hikers, hunters, anglers, mountain bikers, and climbers do what I do and continue to penetrate the last remnants of the grizzly's domain, they place more and more stress on this threatened symbol of the wilderness. Every day it becomes harder and harder for the big bear to avoid us. Fortunately, we can all be part of the solution, instead of part of this problem.

I have confidence that most people interested in going deep into the mountains want to help preserve the king of those mountains, the majestic grizzly bear. That's why we have an obligation to know how to avoid and react to an encounter—because that unfortunate meeting might result in the death of a bear. We should be concerned with our own welfare, of course, but also about the grizzly's tenuous future. Our carelessness can create a "problem bear," which is, of course, a euphemistic name for a soon-to-be-dead bear.

Even worse, perhaps, is the fact that each headline about a bear mauling makes us more afraid of grizzlies and perhaps less certain we want them around. That's why it's so vital for all of us to do all we can to avoid encounters. By doing so, we not only protect ourselves and individual bears, but also help preserve a future for the species.

I also have confidence that anybody who glimpses a wild grizzly will be a strong supporter of wilderness from that moment on. In some cases it might be enough to simply go to where the grizzly walks and sense the presence of the most majestic of animals. Trust me, you can feel it.

The grizzly needs your help. The grizzly needs lots of room, and civilization is gradually nibbling away at the last blank spots on the map. The national parks are not enough. The grizzly needs more than the parks. We also need to accept the bear in large tracts of Western landscape not designated as national parks.

So, in conclusion, the grizzly needs two things from us. The great bear needs all the wild, roadless habitat we have left, and the grizzly needs to be accepted and revered instead of feared or hated. The grizzly needs you.

Acknowledgments

This book is much more than the work of one author.

Through the years I have spent many hours discussing this subject with researchers, wildlife managers, park rangers, and leaders of environmental groups whose names are too numerous to list. I do, however, want to give special thanks to a few of the people who helped me research and review the book: Tom Smith of the Alaska Biological Science Center, Steve Herrero of the University of Calgary, Kerry Gunther of Yellowstone National Park, Gary Moses of Glacier National Park, Bill Stiver of Great Smoky Mountains National Park, Steve Cain of Grand Teton National Park, Christine Cowles of Yosemite National Park, Janet Breau and Mike Grande from Parks Canada, Tom Puchlerz from the Northern Region of the USDA Forest Service, Chris Servheen of the U.S. Fish and Wildlife Service's Interagency Grizzly Bear Team, Chuck Bartlebaugh of the Center for Wildlife Information, bear scientist Chuck Jonkel, and Patti Sowka from the Living with Wildlife Foundation.

The impetus for this book and many of the questions it answers came from the hundreds of people, again too numerous to name, who attended my classes on hiking and camping in bear country at the Yellowstone Institute and other seminars on bear awareness.

I also want to thank the illustrators, Robert Prince and Kirk Botero, and the staff of FalconGuides/Globe Pequot Press for doing such a superb job on the book.

Appendix

Much of the information in this appendix came from the Living with Wildlife Foundation, which contracts with bear managers to keep a current list of manufacturers and sources of bear-resistant products and to coordinate testing and certification protocol. You can find the resource guides online at www.lwwf.org. Contact the foundation at Living with Wildlife Foundation, P.O. Box 1152, Condon, MT 59826; landline (406) 754-0010, cell (406) 544-5307; info@lwwf.org.

Products
Bear Pepper Spray
These companies sell EPA-registered bear deterrent sprays. Manufacturers not registered by the EPA have not been included.

Counter Assault
Counter Assault
120 Industrial Ct.
Kalispell, MT 59901
(800) 695-3394
www.counterassault.com

Frontiersman Bear Attack Deterrent
Security Equipment Corp.
330 Sun Valley Circle
Fenton, MO 63036
(314) 343-2000
www.sabredefensesprays.com

Guard Alaska
McNeil River Enterprises, Inc.
750 West Diamond, Ste. 203
Anchorage, AK 99515
(888) 419-9695
www.guardalaska.com

UDAP Pepper Power
Universal Defense Alternative Products
13160 Yonder Rd.
Bozeman, MT 59715
(800) 232-7941
www.udap.com

Portable Bear-Resistant Food Containers
The Interagency Grizzly Bear Committee has certified the
products of these companies.

Backpacker's Cache
Garcia Machine
14097 Avenue 272
Visalia, CA 93292
(559) 732-3785
www.backpackerscache.com

The Bare Boxer
Golf City Products
9614 Cozycraft Ave. Suite D
Chatsworth, CA 91311
www.bareboxer.com

The Bear Keg
Counter Assault
120 Industry Ct.
Kalispell, MT 59901-7991
(406) 257-4740 or (800) 695-3394
www.counterassault.com

Bear Vault
5663 Balboa Ave. No. 354
San Diego, CA 92111
(866) 301-3442
www.bearvault.com

No Fed Bear Canister
UDAP Industries Inc.
1703 Waterline Rd.
Butte, MT 59701
(800) 232-7941
www.udap.com

Portable Electric Fences
The Interagency Grizzly Bear Committee has certified the
products of these companies.

Bear Shock Fence
UDAP Industries Inc.
1703 Waterline Rd.
Butte, MT 59701
(800) 232-7941
www.udap.com

The Pentagon
Counter Assault
120 Industry Ct.
Kalispell, MT 59901-7991
(406) 257-4740 or (800) 695-3394
www.counterassault.com

Food Hanging Gear
The Interagency Grizzly Bear Committee has certified the products of these companies.

Feather River Bear Bag
(877) 574-2267
www.camping.com

Game Hoist
NATPRO, Inc.
Box 1076
Lander, WY 82520
(307) 332-3068

Hi Stor
Williams Products, Inc.
2825 Rehberg Ln.
Billings, MT 59102
(800) 522-8930

The IGBC website also contains a long list of companies selling bear-resistant garbage containers, panniers, and coolers.

Informational Resources

Books

Backpacker magazine's *Bear Country Behavior,*
  by Bill Schneider
Bear Attacks: Their Causes and Avoidance, by Stephen
  Herrero
Mark of the Grizzly, by Scott McMillion
Where the Grizzly Walks, by Bill Schneider

Videos

Staying Safe in Bear Country and Working in Bear Country,
Safety in Bear Country Society and Wild Eye Productions

Organizations

Be Bear Aware
www.centerforwildlifeinformation.org

Bear Aware
www.bearaware.bc.ca

Get Bear Smart Society
www.bearsmart.com

Interagency Grizzly Bear Committee
www.igbconline.org

Living with Wildlife Foundation
www.lwwf.org

INDEX

A

activity, hours of, 11, 16–17, 19
aggression. *See also* attacks
    behavior signs of, 65, 66
    human acts of, 18, 60
air horns, 80
airplanes, 45, 82
Alaska National Parks, 49–50
alertness, 14–15
alpine-area camping, 37
aluminum foil, 34, 35
ammonia, 57
anglers, 50, 58
animal carcasses, 19–20, 56–57
attacks. *See also* encounters
    black *vs.* grizzly bear
        statistics, 2, 10
    definition, 63
    on dogs, 9–10
    on horses, 11
    on photographers, 18, 60
    preparation and rehearsals
        for, 64
    reaction recommendations
        and options, 49, 64,
        67–71
    survival tips, overview,
        71–73
attractants. *See also* food;
    garbage
    animal carcasses, 19–20,
        56–57
    animal-like sounds, 39
    bear pepper spray, 43–46
    beehives, 76
    bird feeders, 78
    campfire cooking odors,
        11–12
    colors, bright, 39

dog or horse food, 11, 37
dogs, 9–10
elk bugling, 57
fish, 25–26
fruit trees and vegetable
    gardens, 76, 78
human sexual activity, 37
human urine and feces,
    39, 41
menstrual odors, 53–54
scented products, 28, 32,
    39, 53
stove fuels, 35
awareness training, 23, 47, 79, 90

B

backpacks, 20, 28, 33
Banff National Park, 50
bear-detection devices, 82
bear jams, 48–49
bear-resistant food storage
    containers (BRFCs)
    for campsite food storage,
        28, 29, 37
    national park
        requirements, 48, 50,
        51, 52
    sources for, 87–88
    testing programs for, 38
bear sightings, 18, 62, 68
beehives, 76
behavior of bears
    aggression, 65, 66
    as dangerous, 10
    defensive, 63–64, 67–68, 71
    non-defensive (offensive),
        63, 66–70
    predatory, 2, 49, 63, 68–69,
        72

About the Author

Bill Schneider has spent forty years hiking trails all across America. During college in the mid-1960s, he worked on a trail crew in Glacier National Park and became a hiking addict. He spent the 1970s publishing the *Montana Outdoors* magazine for the Montana Department of Fish, Wildlife & Parks, while covering as many miles of trails as possible on weekends and holidays. In 1979 Bill and his partner, Mike Sample, founded Falcon Publishing. Since then, he has written twenty books and hundreds of magazine articles on wildlife, outdoor recreation, and conservation issues.

Bill has also taught classes on bicycling, backpacking, zero-impact camping, and hiking in bear country for the Yellowstone Institute, a nonprofit educational organization in Yellowstone National Park.

In 2000 Bill retired from his position as president of Falcon Publishing (now part of Globe Pequot Press) after it had grown into the premier publisher of outdoor recreation guidebooks, with more than 800 titles in print.

He now lives in Helena, Montana, with his wife, Marnie, and works as a publishing consultant and freelance writer.

For more details, go to www.billschneider.net.